I Like Rain!

Written by Joseph E. O'Day

Illustrated by Ron Foster

Ambassador Books, Inc.
Worcester • Massachusetts

Library of Congress Cataloging-in-Publication Data

O'Day, Joseph E. 1952-
  I like rain / by Joseph E. O'Day ; illustrated by Ron Foster.
      p. cm.
  Summary: A child, who enjoys jumping in puddles, thanks God for rainfall and its beneficial side effects.
  ISBN-13: 978-1-929039-39-5 (hardcover)
  ISBN-10: 1-929039-39-5 (hardcover)
  [1. Rain and rainfall--Fiction. 2. God--Fiction.] I. Foster, Ron, 1950- ill. II. Title.

  PZ7.O2285Iaah 2007
  [E]--dc22

                          2006031429

ISBN-13: 978-1-929039-39-5
ISBN-10: 1-929039-39-5

Published in the United States by Ambassador Books, Inc.
91 Prescott Street • Worcester, Massachusetts 01605
(800) 577-0909

Printed in China.

For current information about all titles from Ambassador Books, visit our website at:
www.ambassadorbooks.com

To my father,
Ralph Jackson O'Day, Sr.

I get excited when it rains
because I LIKE RAIN!

5

I like to watch the big,
black thunderclouds roll
across the sky.

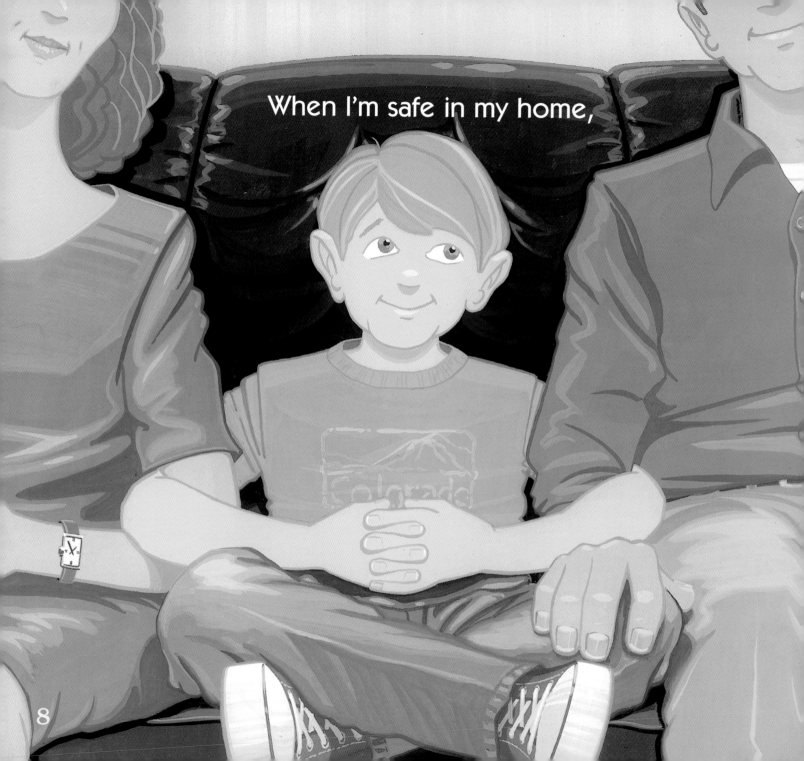

When I'm safe in my home,

I'm not scared of thunder and lightning.
I know it can't hurt me.

When God made the world, thunder
and lightning were part of his plan.

10

Thunder and lightning remind me of how powerful God is. I LIKE RAIN!

11

But lots of people don't like it to rain.

Rain can cause traffic jams because people drive more slowly.

And too much rain can cause floods and even hurt people.

Rain can mess up your hair

15

or get you soaking wet
and chilled to the bone.

But I LIKE RAIN!

God gives me rain so I can have fun!

I like to watch the pouring rain
as it hits the windowpane.

19

I like to run and jump in mud puddles
and see how big a splash I can make.

Sometimes I like
to close my eyes,
tilt my head back,

and feel the rain
hitting my face.

Rain helps fill up the lake
where I swim and
go on boat rides.

I LIKE RAIN!

23

God made rain so I'll
have water to drink.

Rain makes the plants grow so I'll have food to eat.

25

God made rain because he loves me.
I LIKE RAIN!

Whenever it storms,
I remember that God is powerful.

Whenever it rains, I remember that God loves me. I LIKE RAIN!